To Cameron Cowie

From Culduthel Christian Centre
Good News Club.

November 2015

Little Hands
Life of Jesus

Copyright © 2008 Carine Mackenzie
ISBN 978-1-84550-339-0
Reprinted 2009

Christian Focus Publications
Geanies House, Fearn, Tain, Ross-shire, IV20 1TW,
Scotland, United Kingdom
www.christianfocus.com;
email: info@christianfocus.com

Cover design by Daniel van Straaten
Illustrations by Raffaella Cosco

Printed in China

Written with love for
Lydia, Esther and Philip
Lois, Jack, Marianne and Isobel

Contents

Important Announcement

Mary lived in Nazareth, a town in Israel. She was engaged to be married to Joseph, a carpenter.

God sent the angel Gabriel to give Mary important news.

"You are going to have a special baby," he said. "You shall call his name JESUS."

Mary was scared. She could not understand how that could happen.

"Your baby is the Son of God," the angel said. "Nothing is impossible with God."

Mary knew she could trust God. "May everything you have said about me be true," she said. Then the angel left.

In your Bible: Luke 1: 26–38
Question time: What name did God tell Mary to give her baby?
Spot this: How many water pots can you see?

You can be like Mary by believing that Jesus is the Son of God.

To Bethlehem

Joseph was a good man. At first he was troubled when he learned that Mary was expecting a baby. The angel of the Lord appeared to him in a dream.

"Don't be afraid to marry Mary. The baby is God's Son. You will give him the name JESUS (the Saviour) because he shall save his people from their sins."

Joseph and Mary had to make a journey to Bethlehem to enrol in the King's census.

In your Bible: Matthew 1: 18–25
Question time: What does the name Jesus mean?
Spot this: What colour is Mary's dress?

You can be like Joseph by believing God's word.

The Baby is Born

Bethlehem was very busy. When Mary and Joseph arrived there was no room left in the inn. So they found a place to rest for the night where the animals were housed.

That night Mary's baby was born – a boy. She wrapped him up snugly in strips of cloth and laid him in the manger - a wooden box that the animals ate out of.

 In your Bible: Luke 2: 1–7.
Remember this: Where did Mary lay the baby Jesus?
Spot this: What animals can you see in the picture?

You can be like Mary and Joseph by obeying God and doing what he says.

Joyful News

Some shepherds were out in the field that night, taking care of their sheep. An angel of the Lord came and stood by them, shining brightly. They were very afraid.

"I bring you great news." The angel announced. "Today, in the town of Bethlehem, the Saviour has been born. You will find him wrapped up, lying in a manger."

Then a great crowd of angels appeared praising God. "Glory to God in the highest," they said.

 In your Bible: Luke 2: 8–14
Remember this: What good news did the angels bring?
Spot this: How many sheep can you see?

You can be like
the shepherds
by being happy
when you
hear about Jesus.

Shepherds Visit Jesus

When the angels left, the shepherds said to each other, "Let's go to Bethlehem and see for ourselves what has happened."

They hurried along and found Mary and Joseph. There was the baby lying in the manger, just as the angel had said.

After seeing him, the shepherds passed on the good news to everyone they met. They then went back to work, praising God for the wonderful things they had seen and heard.

In your Bible: Luke 2: 15–20
Remember this: Who were the visitors who came to see Jesus?
Spot this: In the picture is it day or night?

You can be like the shepherds by telling God how wonderful he is.

Simeon

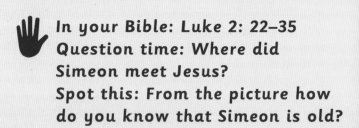

Mary and Joseph took baby Jesus to the temple in Jerusalem when he was about six weeks old. There they offered a sacrifice to God.

A godly old man called Simeon met them in the temple. He was thrilled to see the baby Jesus. He knew that God would send a Saviour one day. Now he believed that he had met God's promised Saviour. He was ready to die. Mary and Joseph were amazed at what Simeon said.

In your Bible: Luke 2: 22–35
Question time: Where did Simeon meet Jesus?
Spot this: From the picture how do you know that Simeon is old?

You can be like Simeon by believing in Jesus for yourself.

Anna

As Simeon was speaking to Mary and Joseph, Anna came along. She had been a widow for a long time.

Now Anna was eighty-four years old and spent all her time in the temple, praying and worshipping God. When she saw the baby Jesus she gave thanks to God for him.

Anna then passed on the good news to all the people who were waiting for the Saviour of God's people.

 In your Bible: Luke 2: 36–39
Question time: What did Anna do when she saw Jesus?
Spot this: What colour of shawl is Anna wearing?

You can be like Anna by spending time with God and then telling others about how lovely Jesus is.

Wise Men

Wise men from an eastern
country came looking for
the new born king. They had
seen a special star in the
sky. The star guided them to Bethlehem and
stopped at the place where Jesus was. They
were so pleased to see the young child.

They brought lovely presents for Jesus
– gold and incense and myrrh. They bowed
down and worshipped him. They knew he
was the promised Saviour – the Son of God.

 **In your Bible: Matthew 2: 1–12
Question Time: What guided the
wise men to Bethlehem?
Spot this: How many camels are
in the picture?**

**Follow Jesus by
obeying God. That is
how you can start
to be wise.**

Journey to Egypt

Joseph was warned by God in a dream to take the young Jesus and his mother to Egypt. It was not safe for them to stay in Bethlehem. Wicked King Herod was jealous of the new born king and wanted to kill him.

After Herod died, the angel appeared in a dream to Joseph in Egypt and told him it was safe to come back. So the family settled in the town of Nazareth.

 In your Bible: Matthew 2: 13–23
Question time: Who was jealous of baby Jesus?
Spot this: What colour is the flamingo?

You can be like Joseph by listening to God and obeying him.

Jesus Grows Up

Jesus grew up in the town of Nazareth. Joseph worked as a carpenter there, making things from wood. Jesus' mother Mary often thought about the wonderful things that had happened at the birth of Jesus.

As he grew older Jesus also grew strong and healthy and wise. He was like no other child. He did not do anything wrong. He always obeyed God's Word.

In your Bible: Luke 2: 39–40
Question time: What work did Joseph do?
Spot this: Can you see a hammer in the picture?

> Trust in Jesus and learn as much as you can about him. There is nobody like Jesus. Jesus has no sin in him at all.

To the Feast

When Jesus was twelve years old, he went with his parents to the temple in Jerusalem for the Passover Feast. Crowds of people came to Jerusalem at that time.

When everyone set off for home, Jesus stayed behind in the temple listening to the teachers and asking questions.

His parents did not miss him at first. They thought he would be with friends in the group. When they could not find him they were anxious.

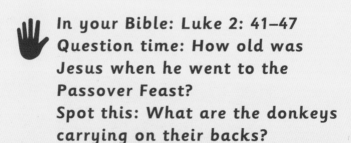

In your Bible: Luke 2: 41–47
Question time: How old was Jesus when he went to the Passover Feast?
Spot this: What are the donkeys carrying on their backs?

Learn to be like Jesus. Listen and learn about God the Father.

In My Father's House

Mary and Joseph returned to Jerusalem looking for Jesus everywhere. At last they found him in the temple. They were astonished to see him talking with the wise teachers.

"Why did you do this to us?" Mary asked. "We have been frantic, looking for you everywhere."

"Did you not know that I must be in my Father's house?" Jesus replied.

Mary and Joseph were puzzled by his reply. Jesus was speaking about God his Father.

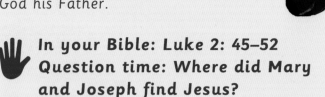

In your Bible: Luke 2: 45–52
Question time: Where did Mary and Joseph find Jesus?
Spot this: Can you see the black and white sheep?

Follow Jesus. Spend time with God, pray to him, trust in him, and love him.

Baptism of Jesus

John had been chosen by God to preach. He told people to turn from their sin to God. Many were baptised in the River Jordan as a sign of turning from sin.

Jesus asked John to baptise him.

"Why do you come to me?" John asked. Jesus had no sins to be washed away. But Jesus insisted.

As he got out of the water, the Holy Spirit came on him in the form of a dove, God the Father spoke from heaven. "This is my beloved Son. I am very pleased with him."

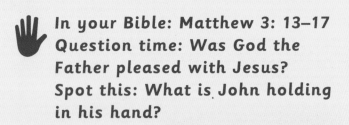

**In your Bible: Matthew 3: 13–17
Question time: Was God the Father pleased with Jesus?
Spot this: What is John holding in his hand?**

You can be like John by turning away from sin and turning to God instead.

First Miracle

Jesus, his mother and his friends were guests at a wedding in Cana. In the middle of the party, Jesus' mother came to him and said, "They have no more wine left." She was sure he could help. "Do what he says," she told the servants.

Jesus told the servants to fill up six big pots with water. Jesus turned the water into the very best wine. This amazing happening is called a miracle. This is the first of many miracles that Jesus did.

In your Bible: John 2: 1–12
Question time: What did the servants put in the big pots?
Spot this: How many water pots can you see?

You can be like Mary by telling others to do what Jesus says.

Nicodemus Visits Jesus

 Nicodemus was a religious leader, who wanted to know more about Jesus and his teaching. One evening after dark he came to speak to Jesus. Jesus told him wonderful truths about God's work and about why Jesus came.

"God loved the world so much," Jesus told him, "that he gave his one and only Son, so that everyone who believes in him will not perish but have eternal life."

 In your Bible: John 3: 1–16 Question time: When did Nicodemus come to see Jesus? Spot this: What is Nicodemus holding?

> You can be like Nicodemus by wanting to know more about Jesus.

Woman of Samaria

Jesus was tired as he walked through Samaria so he stopped for a rest at a well. A woman came at midday to draw water. Jesus spoke to her. He told her about her sinful life. He explained that it was only through himself, Jesus Christ, that she could find the cure to all her problems and needs.

The woman left her water pot and went into town where she told everyone about the man she had met at the well.

"He must be the Christ," she said. "He knew all about me."

Many believed in Jesus that day.

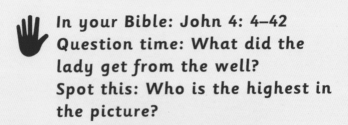

In your Bible: John 4: 4–42
Question time: What did the lady get from the well?
Spot this: Who is the highest in the picture?

You can be like the woman of Samaria by believing in Jesus!

The Nobleman's Son

An important
nobleman heard
that Jesus had
come to a town
near his home.

He went to meet Jesus, to ask him to come
and heal his son. Jesus did not go with him.
He just said to him, "Go home. Your son is
better." The man believed Jesus and went
home. When he arrived he found out that his
boy had begun to get better at exactly the
same time that Jesus spoke to him.

In your Bible: John 4: 46–54
**Question time: Did the father
believe that Jesus could heal his
son?**
**Spot this: What colour is the
boy's cloak?**

You can be like the nobleman by
believing that Jesus does what he says.

The Fishermen

Simon and his brother Andrew were washing their fishing nets on the seashore. Jesus got into Simon's boat and asked him to push it off shore a little. Jesus preached from the boat to the people on the shore.

Afterwards Jesus told Simon to put down his net for a catch of fish. They caught a huge amount of fish.

Jesus asked Simon and Andrew to follow him and become his disciples.

In your Bible: Luke 5: 1–11
Question time: Where was Jesus when he preached?
Spot this: What are the fish being caught in?

You can be like the disciples by following Jesus, and learning from him.

Healing the Sick Lady

 Peter's wife's mother was ill with a raging fever. Jesus came to the house and Peter told him about it.

Jesus took her hand and raised her up. At once the fever left her. Jesus had healed her.

She was completely well and began to serve food to the friends and family.

Many other sick people came to Jesus that evening. He touched them and healed them too.

 In your Bible: Luke 4: 38–40
Question time: What did the lady do as soon as she was cured?
Spot this: What is the lady cooking?

You can be like Peter by telling Jesus all about your problems.

Four Good Friends

 A lame man lay on his mat all day. He could not walk. His four good friends said, "Let's take our friend to Jesus." They carried him on his mat to a house in the town. Jesus was speaking there to a big crowd of people. The friends could not get in.

They climbed up the outside stair, opened up the roof and lowered their friend down in front of Jesus.

"Your sins are forgiven," Jesus said. "Take your mat and go home."

The man was cured.

In your Bible: Mark 2: 1–12
Question time: How many carried the man to Jesus?
Spot this: What colour is the sick man's blanket?

> **You can be like the good friends by asking Jesus to help your friends too.**

Twelve Disciples

Jesus prayed all night on the mountain top. In the morning he gathered his followers and chose twelve men to be apostles. They were to work with him and to preach.

The apostles were Simon Peter, Andrew, James and John, Philip and Bartholomew, Thomas and Matthew, another James and Judas, Simon and Judas Iscariot. These men travelled around with Jesus and learned from him and saw his wonderful work.

✋ **In your Bible: Matthew 10: 2–4**
Question time: How many men did Jesus choose to be disciples?
Spot this: Where is the sun in this picture?

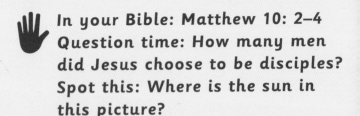

You can be like the disciples by being a follower of Jesus.

Preaching on the Mountain

Jesus was a great teacher. People loved to listen to his preaching. He preached once from a mountainside, teaching many great truths.

"Do not worry," he told his hearers, "Look at the birds. They do not sow or reap crops but God feeds them. You are more precious than them."

It is most important to belong to God and his kingdom.

 **In your Bible: Matthew 5–7
Question time: Who feeds the birds?
Spot this: How many baby birds are there?**

You are like the birds because God looks after them and you.

Soldier's Servant

A Roman soldier sent word to Jesus. "Please come and heal my servant. He is about to die."

When Jesus was nearly at his house, the soldier sent another message. "Please don't come. I am not worthy for you to enter my house. Just say the word and my servant will be healed."

Jesus was amazed at his faith. The servant was healed just as the soldier believed.

✋ **In your Bible: Luke 7: 1–10**
Question time: What message did the soldier send to Jesus?
Spot this: What is the soldier holding?

> You can be like
> the soldier by
> knowing that Jesus
> can be trusted.

A Farmer Sows

Jesus told a story about a farmer sowing seed.

Some seeds fell on the path. The birds ate it.

Some seed fell on rocky ground. It soon withered.

Some seed fell among the thorns. The plant soon died.

Some fell on good ground. It grew well and gave a good harvest.

Jesus' words are like the seed. The person who obeys his word will have a useful and fruitful life.

In your Bible: Matthew 13: 1–9
Question time: What happened to the seed that fell on the path?
Spot this: How many birds are there?

You can be like the good ground if you listen to God's word and obey it.

Calming the Storm

Jesus and his friends sailed across the lake of Galilee. Jesus went to sleep in the stern of the boat. A big storm suddenly came. Waves crashed over the boat. The friends were so scared. They rushed to wake up Jesus.

He spoke to the wind and the sea, "Quiet! Be still." At once there was a great calm.

Jesus had power over the wind and the sea.

In your Bible: Mark 4: 35–41
Question time: What was Jesus doing in the stern of the boat?
Spot this: Can you see the lightning?

Don't be like the disciples who thought Jesus didn't care. Jesus cares for you.

Jairus' Daughter

Jairus' daughter was twelve years old. She became very ill. Her father came to Jesus and begged him to come to his house to heal her. When Jesus reached the house, the girl had died.

Jesus went to her room with her mother and father and his friends Peter, James and John.

"Time to get up, little girl," he said.

She sat up in bed – completely better.

"Give her something to eat now," said Jesus.

In your Bible: Luke 8: 40–56
Question time: What was the girl given when she became well again?
Spot this: Where is the bowl of water?

You can be like Jairus by asking Jesus for help. He is always with us.

Woman of Faith

Lots of people crowded round Jesus. One lady who had been ill for twelve years wanted so much to be healed.

"If I could just touch the hem of his coat," she thought.

As she did that, she was healed of her disease.

"Who touched me?" Jesus asked.

The lady knelt down before him.

Jesus knew she had faith in him.

In your Bible: Mark 5: 25–34
Question time: Which part of Jesus' clothes did the woman touch?
Spot this: Where is the yellow coat?

You can be like the lady by believing in Jesus. He is powerful.

Two Blind Men

Two blind men followed Jesus one day shouting out, "Have mercy on us!"

They followed him into a house.

"Do you believe I can make you see?" asked Jesus.

"Yes, Lord," they replied.

Jesus touched their eyes. Immediately, they could see.

They told everyone they met what Jesus had done.

 In your Bible: Matthew 9: 27–31
Question time: Did the men keep quiet about what Jesus had done?
Spot this: How many walking sticks can you see?

You can be like the blind men by believing that Jesus is always truthful.

Feeding the Crowd

Crowds of people went to listen to Jesus out in the country. By evening they were hungry. Where would they find food?

One little boy had a picnic with him – five small loaves and two fish. Jesus said thank you to God for this food. The disciples handed out the food to the people. Because of Jesus' wonderful power, the little picnic became enough to feed the 5,000 people. There were even twelve baskets left over!

In your Bible: Mark 6: 30–44
Question time: What was in the little boy's picnic?
Spot this: What colour is the lady's dress?

> **You can give Jesus something too. You can give him your love and trust.**

Walking on the Sea

Jesus went to pray in a quiet place alone. His friends sailed across the Sea of Galilee. The wind was against them and the boat was tossed about.

They saw Jesus in the darkness, walking on top of the water. They were so scared.

Jesus called out, "Do not be afraid!"

Peter wanted to go to Jesus on the water. He got out of the boat. When he saw the rough waves, he began to sink. "Lord, save me!" he shouted.

Jesus stretched out his hand to save Peter.

In your Bible: Matthew 14: 22–33
Question time: What did Jesus call out?
Spot this: What bit of Peter's body is in the water?

You can be like Peter by asking Jesus to save you. He will save you from sin.

A Little Child

The disciples were quarrelling about who was the greatest.

Jesus knew they needed to learn an important lesson.

He brought a little child into the group.

"If you want to be great in God's kingdom, you must become as humble as this little child," he said. "These little ones are important to me."

In your Bible: Matthew 18: 1–10
Question time: Why were the disciples quarrelling?
Spot this: Who looks happy in this picture?

You can be humble by putting God and others first before yourself.

The Kind Man

Jesus told this story. He wanted people to understand what a real friend is.

A traveller was robbed and beaten up on a lonely road.

One man came along but hurried past. Another man came. He looked at the injured man, then hurried away too.

Then a kind man rode up on his donkey. He bandaged his wounds, and took him on his donkey to an inn. He looked after him.

Jesus tells us to be like that kind man.

 In your Bible: Luke 10: 25–37 Question time: Where did the kind man take the injured man? Spot this: Where are the bandages?

Jesus wants us to be like the kind man and to help others.

Mary and Martha

The sisters, Mary and Martha loved it when Jesus came to their house.

Mary sat at Jesus' feet, listening to his wise teaching.

Martha was busy preparing the meal.

"Why is Mary leaving me to do all the work?" Martha complained.

"Don't be so worried about serving the food," Jesus said, "Mary is right to spend time listening to me."

In your Bible: Luke 10: 38–42
Question time: Who sat listening to Jesus?
Spot this: Where is Martha's stew pot?

You can be like Mary by spending time listening to God's word.

The Blind Man

Jesus met a man who had been born blind. He had never been able to see.

Jesus made a little mud and put it on the man's eyes.

"Go to the pool of Siloam, and wash it off," he told him.

He came back, able to see for the first time.

The man came to believe that Jesus is the Son of God.

In your Bible: John 9: 1–41
Question time: What did Jesus put on the man's eyes?
Spot this: How many eyes can you see in this picture?

You can be like this man by believing what Jesus says and obeying him.

The Good Shepherd

Jesus wants us to know how much he loves his people. "I am the good Shepherd," Jesus said.

He cares for his people. He loves them so much.

"I will even die for them," he said.

The good shepherd knows his sheep, takes care of them, feeds them and protects them from wild animals and other dangers.

The Lord Jesus knows his people; he feeds them with his Word, the Bible and he protects them from sin.

 **In your Bible: John 10: 1–16
Question time: What does a good shepherd protect his sheep from?
Spot this: How is the shepherd carrying the sheep in this picture?**

You can belong to Jesus.
Thank him for looking after you.

The Lord's Prayer

"Teach us to pray" the disciples asked Jesus one day.

"Pray like this," Jesus said.

"Our Father in heaven hallowed be your name. Your kingdom come. Your will be done, on earth as it is in heaven.

Give us day by day our daily bread.

And forgive us our sins, as we also forgive everyone who sins against us.

Do not lead us into temptation but deliver us from evil."

In your Bible: Luke 11: 1–4
Question time: What did the disciples ask to be taught?
Spot this: How many people can you see in this picture?

You can pray to God. Jesus wants you to spend time with him.

Keep on Praying

Jesus told this story to remind us to keep on praying always.

A friend came to the door, late at night to ask to get some bread for unexpected visitors.

"Go away. It's too late. We are all in bed," said the man.

The friend kept on asking and at last the man got up to give him what he needed.

In your Bible: Luke 11: 5–10
Question time: What did the man do when his friend kept on asking?
Spot this: Who looks annoyed in this picture?

You can always pray to God - anywhere and at anytime.

The Woman with the Bad Back

A lady came to Jesus in the church one Sabbath. She had a bad back and could not even stand up straight.

Jesus called her over, "You are free from your problem now," he told her.

He touched her. Immediately she stood up straight. She was completely better.

She praised God.

 In your Bible: Luke 13: 10–17 Question time: What happened when Jesus touched the lady? Spot this: How can you tell the lady in the picture is happy?

You can be like the lady who was healed by praising God for all his goodness.

The Lost Sheep

Jesus told this story to show God's love and care for one lost sinner.

A shepherd had one hundred sheep to look after. One day a sheep went missing. The shepherd left the other ninety-nine sheep and went to look for the one that was lost. He was so happy when he found it. He had a party with his friends to celebrate.

There is joy in heaven when one lost sinner trusts in Jesus. They are no longer lost. They are found!

 In your Bible: Luke 15: 1–7
Question time: How many sheep went missing?
Spot this: Where is the sheep caught?

You will have joy in your heart when you turn from your sin to Jesus.

The Lost Coin

A lady owned ten precious silver
coins. One day when she counted
her coins, there were only nine.

She lit a lamp and searched the whole
house. She swept into the corners with her
brush.

When she found the missing coin, she was
so happy. She shouted the good news to her
friends.

This story tells about the joy there is in
heaven when a sinner trusts in Jesus and is
found by him.

 **In your Bible: Luke 15: 8–10
Question time: What did the
lady do to search for her coin?
Spot this: Can you see the little
window?**

**You can be like the lady with the coin
when you tell others about Jesus!**

The Lost Son

A loving father was so sad when his youngest son claimed a share of his money and left home to have a good time.

Soon all the money was spent and his new friends did not want to know him anymore. He was lonely and hungry.

"I will go back home. I will ask my father if I can be one of his servants," he thought.

His father saw him coming from a long way off and ran to welcome him home.

God is like the loving father who welcomes sinners to himself.

In your Bible: Luke 15: 11–32
Question time: What did the son want to do when he left home?
Spot this: Who is giving who a hug?

God is like the loving Father. He loves to welcome sinners like us.

Lazarus Falls Sick

Lazarus was very ill. His sisters Martha and Mary decided to send for the Lord Jesus.

When Jesus received the message, he did not immediately go to their house.

Lazarus died. His sisters were so sad and upset.

Martha went to meet Jesus.

"If you had been here, my brother would not have died," she said.

But later Jesus spoke to Lazarus in the tomb and his life was restored.

 In your Bible: John 11: 1–34
Question time: What did Martha and Mary do when their brother became sick?
Spot this: How do you know that these ladies in the picture are feeling sad?

You can be like Martha and Mary. They knew that Jesus could help them.

The Thankful Man

Jesus met ten men on the road. All of them had a serious illness called leprosy.

"Please make us well again," they begged Jesus.

Jesus healed each one of them, as they walked along the road.

Only one came back to Jesus to say thank you.

He praised God as loudly as he could.

"Where are the other nine?" asked Jesus.

How sad that they did not say thank you.

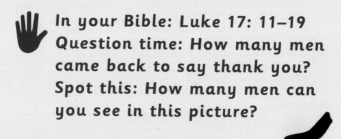

In your Bible: Luke 17: 11–19
Question time: How many men came back to say thank you?
Spot this: How many men can you see in this picture?

You can be like the thankful man if you thank Jesus for all he has done for you.

The Proud Prayer

Jesus told this story to teach that we cannot trust in our own goodness. The only way to God is by trusting in Jesus to forgive our sin.

Two men went to the temple to pray.

An important man prayed, "Thank you that I am not as bad as other people. I do lots of good things."

The other poor man could only say, "God, be merciful to me a sinner."

God didn't think much of the important man's prayer, but he answered the poor man's prayer.

In your Bible: Luke 18: 9–14
Question time: What was the poor man's prayer?
Spot this: In the picture can you point to the man who thinks he is the best?

You can be like the humble man by asking Jesus to save you.

Jesus Loves Children

Mothers and fathers brought their little children to Jesus so that he would bless them.

The disciples tried to turn the children away. Jesus was not pleased with the disciples.

"Let the little children come to me," he said. "Do not stop them. The Kingdom of God belongs to them."

He lifted up the children and blessed them.

 In your Bible: Mark 10: 13–16
Question time: Who tried to turn the children away?
Spot this: How many children can you see?

You can be like these children. Jesus can bless you and give you good things.

Blind Bartimaeus

Poor, blind Bartimaeus sat at
the roadside, begging. One day
he heard that Jesus and his disciples were
coming along the road.

Bartimaeus started to shout, "Jesus, have
mercy on me!"

Some people told him to be quiet, but he
shouted even louder. Jesus called him over.

"What do you want me to do for you?" he
asked.

"I want to see," he replied.

At that moment Jesus healed him and he
could see.

He followed Jesus.

In your Bible: Mark 10: 46–52
**Question time: What did
Bartimaeus want?**
**Spot this: How many coins have
been given to Bartimaeus?**

You can be like Bartimaeus - tell Jesus
what you need. Don't give up!

Zacchaeus

Zacchaeus the tax collector was a cheat. He grew rich by taking more tax money than he should.

Jesus came to his town, Jericho. Crowds lined the street. Zacchaeus was so short he had to climb up a tree to get a good view.

Jesus noticed him. "Come down," he said. "I want to come to your house today."

Zacchaeus was delighted.

"I will repay all the money I stole. I will give away half my things to poor people."

Zacchaeus' life was changed by meeting Jesus.

In your Bible: Luke 19: 1–10
Question time: How did Zacchaeus get to see Jesus?
Spot this: How many laughing boys can you see in the picture?

> **You can be like Zacchaeus by being sorry for your sins.**

Mary and the Ointment

Jesus came to Simon's house for a meal. Lazarus, whom Jesus had raised from the dead, was at the table too.

Martha was busy as usual serving the food.

Mary took a very expensive jar of ointment and poured it over Jesus' head and feet. She wiped his feet with her hair.

"What a waste," complained Judas.

"Leave her alone," said Jesus. "She has done a good thing."

Mary did this to show how much she loved Jesus. She gave him her most precious possession.

In your Bible: John 12: 1–11
Question time: What did Mary pour over Jesus' head and feet?
Spot this: Is the vase that Mary is holding spotted or striped?

You can be like Mary by showing others that you love Jesus.

Donkey Ride to Jerusalem

Jesus sent two of his disciples to borrow a young donkey. "The Lord needs it," they told the owners. They put clothes on the donkey's back and Jesus sat on it.

A very large crowd spread their coats and palm branches on the road. He rode into the city of Jerusalem.

The people shouted praise to God as they walked along the road.

The journey into Jerusalem caused great interest.

In your Bible: Matthew 21: 1–11
Question time: What did the people spread on the road?
Spot this: Where is the little boy in the picture?

You can be like the cheering crowds by singing about how great God is.

The Last Supper

Jesus and his disciples ate a special meal together in an upstairs room. Jesus took some bread, blessed it and broke it in pieces.

"Take this and eat it," he said to them. "This is like my body which will soon be broken for you."

Jesus knew he was soon going to suffer and die for his people. He passed round a cup of wine. "Drink this. It is like my blood."

Jesus was speaking about his dying for sinners.

In your Bible: Matthew 26: 26–29
Question time: Where did Jesus eat this special meal?
Spot this: What colour is the wine in the glass?

When you see bread and wine - remember that Jesus died to save his people.

Jesus Washes Feet

After supper Jesus poured some water into a basin and washed his disciples' feet. He wiped them with a towel.

Lowly servants usually did this job. But their Lord and Master Jesus was willing to serve them.

"You should serve each other in the same way," he told them.

In your Bible: John 13: 1–17
Question time: Who did the job of a servant in this story?
Spot this: Point to all the shoes in the picture?

Learn to be like Jesus. Treat others as more important than you.

Jesus and Peter

After supper they all went out to the Mount of Olives.

"You will be ashamed of me tonight," Jesus told them.

"I will never be ashamed of you," replied Peter.

"I am telling you Peter," said Jesus, "that before the cockerel crows in the morning you will deny three times that you even know me."

"I would never do that," said Peter boldly. He did not know how weak he was.

In your Bible:
Mark 14: 26–31
Question time: Did Peter think that he would deny Jesus?
Spot this: What is Peter standing beside?

You might be like Peter if you think you know better than God. Watch out!

Garden of Gethsemane

Jesus and the disciples then went to the Garden of Gethsemane.

Jesus asked Peter and James and John to be on watch while he went to pray. Jesus was very sad. He knew he would soon die.

Jesus prayed to God the Father alone. Peter, James and John fell asleep. They did not keep watch for even one hour.

In your Bible: Mark 14: 32–42
Question time: What did Jesus do in the garden?
Spot this: Are the men sleeping inside or outside?

Are you like the disciples? Do you want to learn more about God or do you give up?

Betrayed

Judas Iscariot arrived with a crowd of men carrying swords.

Judas was not a real friend of Jesus.

He went up to him and said, "Master" and kissed him. This was the sign for the soldiers to grab Jesus and take him away.

Judas Iscariot had betrayed Jesus.

All the disciples ran away and left Jesus alone.

In your Bible: Mark 14: 43–52
Question time: Did any of the disciples stay with Jesus?
Spot this: How many spears can you see?

Are you a real friend of Jesus? Do you obey him even if it is hard to?

The Trial

Jesus was led away to the palace of Caiaphas, the High Priest.

The officials wanted to find out something against Jesus. They hated him and wanted to kill him. They could find nothing against him. Many told lies about him.

Jesus kept silent. He did not answer back.

"Are you the Christ, the Son of the Blessed?" the High Priest asked him.

"I am," he replied.

They all condemned him to death.

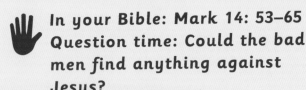

In your Bible: Mark 14: 53–65
Question time: Could the bad men find anything against Jesus?
Spot this: What colour is the priest's scarf?

You can be like Jesus by telling the truth, even when other people tell lies.

Denial

Peter followed Jesus at a distance right into the palace.

In the courtyard a servant girl recognised Peter. "You were with Jesus," she said.

"I don't know what you are talking about," he replied.

In the porch another girl said he had been with Jesus.

Again he denied this.

Then another person said to him, "You must be one of Jesus' followers."

Roughly Peter said, "I do not know the man."

 In your Bible: Mark 14: 66–71
Question time: Where did Peter follow Jesus to?
Spot this: How are the people in the picture staying warm?

You might be like Peter if you are afraid to follow Jesus. Watch out!

The Cockerel Crows

Just then the cockerel crew.

Jesus turned round and looked at Peter.

He remembered what Jesus had said to him.

"Before the cockerel crows, you shall deny me three times."

Peter had denied his Master. He went outside and wept bitterly.

Jesus was tied up and taken to the ruler Pilate.

 In your Bible: Matthew 26: 74–75
Question time: How many times had Peter denied that he knew Jesus?
Spot this: What is the cockerel standing on?

You might be like Peter if you don't believe Jesus. Watch out!

Pilate

Pilate the governor questioned Jesus.

"Are you the King of the Jews?"

"My kingdom is not of this world," replied Jesus.

"I find no fault with Jesus," Pilate said.

The crowd shouted out, "Crucify him, crucify him!"

Pilate gave in and sent Jesus to be crucified.

In your Bible: John 19: 1–16
Question time: Could Pilate find any fault with Jesus?
Spot this: How many people are in this picture?

Don't always do what everyone else does. Do the right thing. Follow Jesus.

Crucifixion

Jesus was cruelly treated.

The soldiers made a crown of thorns and jammed it on his head.

They mocked him. They spat on him. They beat him with sticks.

They took him to Calvary and nailed him to a cross of wood.

The soldiers took his clothes and played a game to see who would win the clothes for themselves.

Jesus prayed to God, "Father, forgive them, for they do not know what they are doing."

 In your Bible: Luke 23: 26–38
Question time: Where was Jesus nailed to a cross?
Spot this: Can you see the whip?

You can be like Jesus by forgiving those people who are mean to you.

Two Robbers

Two robbers were crucified with Jesus — one on each side of him.

One of them complained to Jesus, "Why can't you save us?"

The other said, "We deserve to be here, but Jesus has done nothing wrong.

Remember me when you come to your kingdom," he asked Jesus.

Jesus replied, "Today you will be with me in heaven."

That man trusted in Jesus just as he was dying. The other robber did not trust.

In your Bible: Luke 23: 39–43
Question time: Who was crucified with Jesus?
Spot this: What are the people using to spot the robber in the dark?

You might be like the forgiven thief by trusting that Jesus can save you.

It is Finished

Jesus cried out from the cross, "It is finished." Then he died.

Why did he die? Was it just because bad men hated him? No, it wasn't.

Jesus died because God must punish sin. Jesus took that punishment himself in the place of people who trust in him.

Boys and girls who trust in Jesus, have all their sins forgiven. Jesus means Saviour. He came to "save his people from their sins."

On the cross this work was finished.

 In your Bible: John 19: 29–30
Question time: What words did Jesus cry out from the cross?
Spot this: How many crosses can you see?

You can see how loving Jesus is. He was willing to die to save sinners!

In the Grave

Jesus' body was laid in a grave. A big stone was placed over the entrance.

Some ladies who loved Jesus went to the grave early in the morning. They found that the stone had been rolled away.

They could not find the body of the Lord Jesus.

Two angels spoke to them. "He is not here. He has risen."

The ladies rushed to tell the disciples what had happened.

In your bible: Mark 16: 1–8
Question time: What did the angels say to the ladies?
Spot this: How many ladies can you see?

You can be like these women by loving Jesus and telling others he is alive!

Jesus Appears

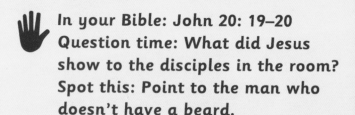

The disciples were scared and sad. They met together in a room with the doors tightly shut.

They were afraid of being killed too.

Then Jesus appeared in the room.

"Peace be to you," he said.

Jesus showed them his hands which had been pierced by the nails on the cross, and his side which had been pierced by a spear.

The disciples were now so glad because Jesus had risen from the dead and come to see them.

In your Bible: John 20: 19–20
Question time: What did Jesus show to the disciples in the room?
Spot this: Point to the man who doesn't have a beard.

You can be like the disciples by being glad about how Jesus defeated death!

At Sea of Galilee

Peter and six other disciples went fishing on the Sea of Galilee. They caught nothing.

When morning came, they saw a man watching them from the shore.

"Have you any food?" he called.

"No," they replied.

"Put the net out on the right side of the boat and you will find fish."

John realised that the man was Jesus.

"It is the Lord," he said to Peter.

Peter dived into the water to reach the shore as soon as possible.

 In your Bible: John 21: 1–7
Question time: What did Peter and the others do on the sea of Galilee?
Spot this: What bit of Peter's body is in the water?

> **You can be like John by telling others who Jesus is.**

Breakfast on the Shore

The disciples sailed to the shore dragging the net full of fish behind them.

Jesus had a meal of fish and bread waiting for them.

"Come and eat breakfast," he invited them.

They knew that he was the risen Lord Jesus.

Jesus spoke encouraging words to Peter who had denied him. He forgave him and wanted him to preach the gospel.

In your Bible: John 21: 8–19
Question time: What had Jesus prepared for breakfast?
Spot this: How many fish are being cooked?

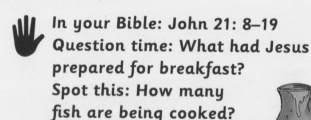

You can be like Peter. Jesus forgave his mistakes. He can forgive you too.

Road to Emmaus

Cleopas and his friend were walking back home to Emmaus.

A man came alongside them, and asked them. "Why are you so sad?"

"Have you not heard what has happened? We thought Jesus would save our country but he has been killed. His body is not in the tomb. We don't know what has happened."

The man then explained to them from the Bible how Christ had to suffer.

The man went into the house with them and only then did they realise that he was Jesus himself. Jesus then disappeared from their sight.

In your Bible: Luke 24: 13–32
Question time: Who was walking with Cleopas and his friend?
Spot this: Point to the food and the drink in this picture.

> **You can be like Cleopas. Pray to Jesus. Jesus will teach you too.**

Through the Clouds

Jesus and his disciples were on the Mount of Olives outside Jerusalem.

"Very soon," Jesus told them, "God will send the Holy Spirit to you. He will help you to tell the good news about me in many places."

After he said this, Jesus was taken up to heaven. Soon the clouds hid him from view.

God the Holy Spirit helped Peter and the other disciples to preach the gospel to many people - the good news that Jesus came to this world and died on the cross for sinners. Boys and girls who trust in Jesus, have all their sins forgiven.

In your Bible: Acts 1: 1–11
Question time: What good news did Peter preach?
Spot this: How many boats can you see in this picture?

You can be like Peter. You can tell the world about Jesus!

Bible Passages

CHRISTIAN FOCUS PUBLICATIONS

Christian Focus | Christian Heritage | CF4K | Mentor

Christian Focus Publications publishes books for adults and children under its four main imprints: Christian Focus, CF4K, Mentor and Christian Heritage. Our books reflect that God's word is reliable and Jesus is the way to know him, and live for ever with him.

Our children's publication list includes a Sunday School curriculum that covers pre-school to early teens; puzzle and activity books. We also publish personal and family devotional titles, biographies and inspirational stories that children will love.

If you are looking for quality Bible teaching for children then we have an excellent range of Bible story and age specific theological books.

From pre-school to teenage fiction, we have it covered!

Find us at our web page:
www.christianfocus.com

CF4•K
*Because you're never
too young to know Jesus*